T(

W:

MW01233230

appreciation and love
for who you are!

Sandra

2020

Straight Talk
for

COLLEGE-BOUND STUDENTS

and

Their Parents

WHAT NO ONE TELLS YOU
BUT EXPECTS YOU TO KNOW

SAUNDRA RICHARDSON MCKAY

STRAIGHT TALK FOR COLLEGE-BOUND
STUDENTS AND THEIR PARENTS
WHAT NO ONE TELLS YOU BUT
EXPECTS YOU TO KNOW

iUniverse books may be ordered through booksellers or by contacting:

*iUniverse
1663 Liberty Drive
Bloomington, IN 47403
www.iuniverse.com
1-800-Authors (1-800-288-4677)*

*Because of the dynamic nature of the Internet, any web addresses or
links contained in this book may have changed since publication and
may no longer be valid. The views expressed in this work are solely those
of the author and do not necessarily reflect the views of the publisher,
and the publisher hereby disclaims any responsibility for them.*

*Any people depicted in stock imagery provided by Getty Images are
models, and such images are being used for illustrative purposes only.
Certain stock imagery © Getty Images.*

*ISBN: 978-1-5320-9110-0 (sc)
ISBN: 978-1-5320-9109-4 (e)*

Library of Congress Control Number: 2020900325

Print information available on the last page.

iUniverse rev. date: 01/08/2020

To the many students and parents I had the honor of serving during my thirty-five years and who taught and molded me along the way. I enjoyed being a part of your successes!

To my husband, Bruce, who encouraged me to write this book and stood beside me with loving support. To my children, whom I cherish dearly, Dana, Edward, Brucie, Aaron, and Skylar, and my host of adorable grands and great-grands! Thank you, Sabrina.

Acknowledgments

The following are colleges and universities that I have been affiliated with during my tenure in higher education:

Richmond Community College
University of North Carolina at Pembroke
Sandhills Community College
University of Evansville
University of Houston–Clear Lake
University of Houston–Fort Bend
Houston Community College System
Queens College–Charlotte, North Carolina
University of North Carolina at Chapel Hill

Introduction

In 1989, at Queens College, a small, upscale, private women's institution in Charlotte, North Carolina, I interviewed for the position of student development coordinator. On a cool January afternoon, I met with the vice president of academic affairs and confirmed and accepted the position. As student development coordinator, I would be her assistant, and my job would be to connect with the student population and find out from them if they were happy there, and if they weren't, why not. What was working and what was not?

I had no idea how to do that or where to begin. I had no experience with that sort of thing and had been chosen by the student government association because they felt comfortable with me after meeting with them on two separate occasions.

I was given an old office with an old, dusty desk, a chair, and a bookcase with one book on the shelf. The huge letters on the big black book read NACADA. It looked like it was a hundred years old. I didn't have a clue what the letters meant.

Again I met with the vice president to gather more information about how and where to begin introducing myself to the college, especially since this was a new position. She shared that I was to attend meetings with her that involved the faculty, to learn what the role of the faculty was. I would also attend meetings involving anything that had to do with students at the college. She gave me a college catalog and said, "Know this book from cover to cover. Your job is to help students navigate their way to graduation within the guidelines of this book. Find the pitfalls and show them how to get around them." That was the beginning of my new life as a student advocate.

My goal in this book is to share the things no one tells students but expects them to know when entering college. Many students entering colleges and universities have no clue how those institutions work. Nor do they know what's expected of them and where to find these secrets. Many students are unaware that planning for college begins early, in middle school and junior high school—definitely before you enter high school.

I will share with you the secrets I have learned during thirty-five years of helping students navigate the complex system of higher education. By the end of this book, you will know the shortcuts and secrets for entering college and completing your diploma. Like I was always told, take what you can use from this book and discard what you may already know.

I will share information about two-year colleges and four-year colleges and universities. I have experience in both, as well as private institutions.

This book is set up to guide students and parents through the middle grade and high school years in preparation for entering college. I will discuss the courses to enroll in, the skills that students should develop early, and the conversations parents should have with their students.

Knowing what my students' struggles have been in managing their challenges each semester, I will discuss what stands out as areas of special importance while pursuing a higher education. The research data about today's college student is also included.

PART

I

Are Students Ready for College?

According to the Association of Colleges and Universities, "The hard truth is that success in college is strongly related to precollege academic preparation and achievement as well as other factors such as family income and parents' education." Students who do not attain grade-level proficiencies in math and reading by the eighth grade are much less likely to be college ready at the end of high school. Along with college-level academic skills, high school students must also develop study habits and other behavioral patterns associated with postsecondary success. Once students start college, engaging in effective education practices can increase their chances for success.

"Although the vast majority of high school seniors (more than 90 percent) say they intend to go on to postsecondary education, many do not engage in the kinds of educational activities that will prepare them to do well in college" (McCarthy and Kuh 2006).

Plan for College Early

Regardless of whether it's a two-year or four-year college, plan, plan, plan. Don't wait until your eleventh- or twelfth-grade year to begin thinking about college. If you do, you will be far behind. At least by eighth grade, you should have a plan for what you will do once you graduate high school. Not everyone attends college. Some seek employment immediately after graduating, with no experience and little education. Some attend a two-year college for the technical classes, and others want to continue their education through the undergraduate and graduate levels. If the latter describes you, then prior to entering high school, you must know the courses to enroll in while in high school that will prepare you for college.

Most colleges and universities prefer that you have completed the following:

- English—four years
- math—four years
- science—three years
- foreign language—two years
- social studies—one year
- history—one year
- electives—one year
- high school grade point average—3.72 (at least)

You should take challenging classes in high school, as listed above. Fluff courses will not prove valuable if you want to be prepared for college. Always keep up with your grade point average as each year ends, because colleges will want you to list your grade point average from high school on your college application.

Also, if you enroll in AP (Advanced Placement) courses and take the CLEP (College-Level Examination Program), retain the copy of your grades from the College Board so that you can give them to the registrar at the college you will be applying to. This is something students are not aware of. The scores on your copy of these exams will tell you if you have scored high enough to receive credit in college level courses. For example, if you receive a high enough score in biology, you will not need to enroll in that class; you will be exempt. That is why the registrar must have a copy of the grades you received from the College Board *before* you register for classes, so that you don't take a class you don't need. By the way, each college catalog has a page devoted to Advanced Placement and CLEP, showing the scores needed, the name of the course, and the hours awarded. Check it out. This is another way of saving time and money.

Once you begin to think about what careers you are interested in and the types of jobs that pique your interest, do your research and find out more about what major you should pursue to meet the qualifications for that job or career. Most students approach this backward. They select colleges without knowing if the colleges have their particular degrees. They are so anxious to attend a certain college, they don't check if their majors are listed until they get there, and then they struggle to figure out what to do.

So, while you are in junior high and high school, do your research to figure out what you would like to be when you grow up and look for colleges that cater to that particular area of expertise. Then research what you will need to do while in college to graduate and attain that degree.

I said earlier that at my first job, I was told to learn the college catalog from front to back in order to help students around the pitfalls and lead them to graduation. Today, the college catalog of each institution is online for your viewing. I personally feel it's tough to navigate online through the many pages of a catalog to find what you really need to know when entering college. Yes, I am old school, and I love the hard copy of a catalog, so I can mark the pages with what I need to keep up with. Some things you will learn as you go, but there are certain things you need to know before you apply.

Develop a College Plan

A college plan is a step-by-step guide for the requirements that will prepare you for a career in your area of interest. In developing a college plan, you must have an idea of the areas you are interested in pursuing. What do you see yourself doing one day? What does it take to be that person? What are your strengths and weaknesses? I wanted to pursue nursing until I realized that I was not strong in science and math, and those are a must for a career in nursing. So, I had to rethink my options—and quickly.

At what type of college (two-year/four-year), according to your career choices, are you planning to pursue your dream? Do you know the colleges that hold the degree program that you are planning to pursue? Have you researched the courses that are required for you to complete the degree? It's important to make a plan and research what lies ahead so that you can be successful. Always have a backup plan in case you change your direction along the way.

As part of your plan, make sure you include important dates. You must know the upcoming dates required for you to move forward and complete each step. Listed here are a few examples. Mark your calendar with important dates for the following:

- – college application deadlines (high school transcript included)
- – SAT/ACT deadlines to register and take exams
- – letters of recommendation
- – college visits (tour the campuses of your choice)
- – college orientation and registration

Two-Year College

In a two-year college, you will pursue a technical degree that will allow you to enter into the workforce in two years or less. Examples of jobs attainable with this degree are nursing assistant, welder, HVAC technician, and certified management accountant (CMA). But you can also attend a two-year institution to prepare to transfer to a four-year college. Be careful! Let me give you the inside scoop about attending a two-year college in preparation for transferring to a four-year institution.

If you would like to save time and money, enroll in a two-year college, in a two-year program designed to transfer to a four-year college. You must apply and register this way at the very beginning of enrolling in a two-year college. Why? Two-year colleges are designed for all entering students to pursue and complete a two-year degree. You do not have to complete a degree at a two-year college in order to transfer to a four-year college. And if you do complete the two-year degree prior to transferring, you will find that most of your courses will not transfer to the four-year institution. This fact has turned parents and students against attending two-year colleges for years. They sum it up as a waste of time and money. But they did not do their research prior to enrolling. If you apply and register for *the two-year transfer program*, this program will sign you up for classes that will transfer to a four-year college. There are academic advisors there to guide you through this process. You will be on the transfer track from the beginning, and the advisor will be advising you according to the college requirements of the four-year college that you plan to attend.

By taking the correct courses while you are at the two-year college, you can transfer in as a junior, meaning you will have completed your freshman and sophomore years at the two-year institution. Once you have completed your courses, you then transfer to the four-year college of your choice and continue your requirements for the degree. You are not required to take the ACT/SAT to enroll in a two-year institution as you are for the four-year institution. So, there are perks to attending both institutions.

The two-year institution will require you to take a placement test in order to determine if you are ready for college-level English and math, and if not, you will be enrolled in developmental courses to prepare you for the college level. These courses do not count toward graduation.

Once you enter college-level courses, make sure your grade in each course is not below a C. Grades below a C will not transfer. You may not understand this now, but you will eventually. Grades don't transfer; hours transfer. For example, if you complete English with a grade of A, earning you three semester credit hours, the three semester hours of credit will transfer, meaning your grade of A meets the criteria of the college you are transferring to.

Four-Year College

Here are few terms to be familiar with when applying to college: first-generation student, nontraditional student, undeclared student, and transfer student.

First-Generation Students

First-generation students are the first people in their families to attend college. These students usually have little family support to guide them in preparing for college and in helping them understand what will be expected of them when they enroll. This is important for a few reasons. There are college scholarships that are set aside for the first-generation student, to assist with financial obligations to the institution. If you are a first-generation student, you will need a support system right away. In an article in *Peer Review*, "First-Year Reflections," Carol Sun shows a high percentage of these students withdraw from college the first semester because they have difficulty navigating the system, have limited knowledge, and do not seek the right office on campus to assist them. There are advisors available to assist with this population, but the students must be aware that they fit into this category so that they can receive all the benefits.

Some campuses provide programs for first-generation students through TRIO, a federally funded government program established by the 1965 Higher Education Act. The three prominent programs under TRIO are Upward Bound, Talent Search, and Student Support Services. TRIO offers mentoring and career counseling and can help students at two-year colleges transfer to a four-year college. The advisor-student relationship allows the student to feel more at home on the campus and be better equipped to deal with the stresses of being the first in the family to obtain a degree in higher education.

Nontraditional Students

Nontraditional students are beginning or continuing their education at a later-than-typical age. They have delayed college for a year or more following high school, are single parents with dependents, are employed full-time, are financially independent, or are attending part-time.

Colleges and universities have attempted to create programs and services that are responsive to nontraditional students and their learning preferences. These students should seek out adult-oriented programs and services on their campuses for student support. The design and delivery of these programs are key to successful undergraduate experiences for reentry adult students. More than half of nontraditional students transfer in after attending a community college and being away from the classroom for a while. They may not have declared their majors, or they may have chosen their courses haphazardly and interrupted their studies because they ran out of money, had to change jobs, joined the military, or had other circumstances.

For adult students, that delay in transferring credit can come at a disastrous cost. They may waste tuition dollars on courses that are redundant or enroll in courses that are beyond their levels of preparation. This can be very discouraging and include unnecessary expense.

While adults are mature and motivated, some return to the classroom unsure of their capacity or preparation for college-level coursework. And, because of embarrassment, they are less likely to ask for help when they need it most. Resources are available, which I will cover later in this book, but you must take advantage of them.

Finally, research shows that adult students flock to online courses because of their flexibility. But don't forget the social and community connections that might be built in a face-to-face environment.

Undeclared Students

Undeclared students are not yet sure of their career paths and what they would like to declare as their majors. Know that it's okay if you have not determined your major upon entry. You have at least a year and a half to do so. Most schools would prefer you to enter undeclared so that you have time to research and do not find yourself jumping in and out of majors. But please note that there are some majors that start freshman year; in that case, you must make sure you have the groundwork of your major early.

Transfer Students

Transfer students are students who have earned twenty-four or more semester hours and have decided to leave their current schools and attend two-year or four-year institutions. There are requirements for entering a school after leaving another. First, to transfer, you must have the required number of semester hours, which is generally a minimum of twenty-four hours, with a minimum grade point average of 2.0. The new school will evaluate the courses you have taken and decide which courses they will accept at their institution. Please pay close attention to this evaluation so there won't be any surprises later.

There are two ways to apply and get admitted to a four-year institution. You can enroll as a freshman or transfer in as an upperclassman. To enroll as a freshman, you must take the ACT/SAT test, complete an application, and submit letters of recommendation and your high school transcript. Deadlines for admission are important!

If you are a transfer student, you must also submit an application and a transcript from the prior school with no less than a 2.0 grade point average. Remember, no grades lower than a C will transfer.

If you are entering as a freshman at a four-year school, you will be expected to attend an orientation for new students. This is also when you will register for your classes. Usually, you will meet with an academic advisor who will guide you through this process. Ask plenty of questions as your schedule of classes is being compiled. You definitely have a say in your class schedule. Are you an early-morning person, or do you prefer your classes in the afternoon? As a freshman, your classes will be general education classes that are required for all students graduating in any degree program, such college English, math, and science. Some classes are only offered in the early morning during your freshman year, so your choices may be few as far as the time is concerned. Once your schedule is complete, hang on to it until you know exactly where your classes are located and the times of the classes. Knowing where your classes are located will help you estimate the time you have between classes to make it to the next class on time. Classes fill up quickly, so get your class schedule finalized as quickly as you can. Sometimes you may have to wait until the following semester for a class if the class closes before you sign up. There are several orientations during registration time, so try to sign up for the earliest orientation session.

Once you have registered for classes, attend your first class in each subject before you purchase your textbook. Know the return policy in case you want to return a book because you decided not to take that class. Keep all receipts!

If you are a transfer student, go to orientation. You may have attended orientation at the prior school, but this is a new school with new people, a new location, and new rules. You need to know certain things, such as where to park and where the resources are if you need assistance, and you need to be able to put a name with a face. Each school is different, so taking time to attend an orientation will be useful to you. There are orientations set up specifically for transfer students who are upperclassmen. Believe me, it is not a waste of your time.

As a transfer student, an evaluation of your course credits will be done by your new school. Make sure you have a copy of your evaluation with you when you register for classes. You need that evaluation so that you don't register for classes that you already have credit for. Believe me, that happens, and it's a waste of time and money.

If you are planning to live on campus, make sure you check in with housing for your room assignments, roommate assignments, and so on. If you are allowed to bring your car, check out the rules and regulations and where you can and cannot park. Personally, I feel that freshmen should not bring a car their first year. You have too much to learn about college to have the headache of figuring out where to park and getting parking tickets when space is not available.

Academic Advisors

Academic advisors and professional advisors are part of the support system assigned to students to assist them through graduation. Institutions are aware that systems must be in place to address the needs of students, especially in the changing nature of the term *freshman* as the number of nontraditional, older, married, and working students continues to increase.

Each student is assigned an academic advisor. Whether you are a new freshman or a transfer student, you will be assigned an advisor. Know who that person is and where he or she is located. The advisor is your first line of contact if you need something. If you are a freshman, you will meet with this person to register for classes each semester, until you declare a major. Once you have declared a major, you will be assigned an advisor in the department of your major.

If you are a transfer student, you will be assigned an advisor in your major. As a transfer student, by the time of enrollment, you should know what you are majoring in, so having an advisor in your major should be a priority at this point in your college career.

Your advisor is there to guide you along each semester in registering you for the appropriate classes through graduation. You will need to make sure you are taking the correct classes each semester and look over your advisor's shoulder to make sure he or she is giving you accurate information. You do that by having your own copy of the college catalog and a major course sheet that outlines what courses you will take each semester. Make sure you have taken the prerequisites before you enroll in your classes. I will discuss prerequisites later. Department advisors are good at telling you what courses to register for in your major, but they are not necessarily accurate when it comes to the requirements and policies in general education. I know because, as director of academic advising for many years, I have seen many mistakes made by professors who are selected to be advisors in their majors. They do a poor job. That's why when a student finds a good advisor, the student holds on to that person for dear life! I was one of those advisors. And I never turned a student away, because I know how critical it is to graduate on time. I was also a registrar at one point in my career, and I had to be the bearer of bad news when students thought they were graduating but were a credit short.

If you are undecided about your major, there is usually a support center or advising center where you can find assistance. By the time you have completed your general education courses, you should be ready to declare your major. Remember, in order to graduate on time, you should be completing a set number of courses each semester. Do not get in the habit of enrolling in classes and withdrawing before the end of the semester. That habit will hurt you academically and financially. To keep this from happening, you need a signature from your advisor in order to withdraw from a class. And if you must withdraw from a class, there is a deadline each semester for permission to do so. Please keep your copy of the withdrawal slip.

Importance of the College Catalog

Each college/university, whether two-year, four-year, public, or private, publishes a catalog. I prefer the hard copy, but these days, institutions publish their catalogs online. During my thirty-five years in higher education, I always kept a copy of the catalog and taught my students to do the same.

Why is it so important? Let me list a few reasons that you may not be aware of.

- The academic year that you enrolled at the institution is posted on the cover. This is important to you because institutions publish a new catalog every one or two years. Any changes made in the upcoming catalogs will not affect you as long as you are attending each semester consecutively. Changes are generally made at the beginning of the fall semester. So, if you withdraw during the spring semester and return the next fall, you may be placed under a new catalog, which may have different requirements than your previous catalog. Students will not be able to meet some of the requirements in one catalog and some of the requirements of another catalog. So, know the catalog year you began your studies.

— The academic calendar for the year is included in the catalog. Why is this calendar important? All of the important dates for the fall and spring semester are posted for students. For example, it includes the date of the first day of classes; the last day to drop and add classes; the deadline for immunizations; all holidays that are observed by the institution; fall and spring breaks; the last day to withdraw from a class; final exams; when to register for the next semester; and when to apply for graduation. You must apply when you are ready to graduate. Once you are close to graduation, know that date!

What Is a College Catalog?

Each institution has a catalog or handbook that provides the following information:

— a list of all the academic services and facilities that are available to you
— the undergraduate programs that are available at the institution and their requirements
— the general education requirements for all students, along with the names of the courses and the number of hours required

- academic policies, including the grading system and how to add, drop, and withdraw from a class; registration procedures and policies; grade replacement policy; withdrawal from the institution policies; independent study policies; class attendance policies; FERPA policies; academic honor code; and what to expect from faculty
- undergraduate admissions information about scores for CLEP and Advanced Placement, financial aid, scholarships, loans, grants, and how each of these are affected when you withdraw from a course
- information about student affairs, student housing and residence life, student health services, career services, Greek life, student conduct, police and public safety, parking and vehicle registration, students' rights and responsibilities, and the code of conduct

Each semester, I taught a course called Freshman Seminar. In this course, I gave each student a copy of the college catalog, and they were required to read and explain to the class the sections of the catalog that were assigned to them. They made the information exciting, and it was such an eye-opening experience for them that they passed what they learned to other students on campus. And when they visited the offices on campus, they knew what to expect when handling their business.

Other Information You Need to Know

First-Year Seminar / University 101

First-Year Seminar, sometimes referred to as University 101, is a course designed to assist students during the first semester as they adjust to college life. This course teaches you where resources are located on campus and how to utilize them. Each student receives a copy of the college catalog. Know that the catalog is a contract between you and the school. And please know what the terms are in case you find yourself in a situation and you need a way out. Remember, I told you earlier that my job was to assist students around the pitfalls.

Graduation Requirements

My advisor in college was a godsend to me. I was too busy trying to keep my head above water to keep up with the policies and regulations from semester to semester. So, I relied on him to keep me up to speed regarding which courses to enroll in from semester to semester.

When graduation time came, I received what was called a "quickie note" from the registrar's office about a one-hour requirement that was not found on my transcript of classes taken during my four and a half years. I was a music major, and it was the most difficult major to follow when counting all the requirements semester to semester. Well, my advisor knew exactly where their counting was off and made a call to the registrar's office, showing them the requirement that completed my studies. Whew! That's what you *don't* need at graduation time. This is one of the main reasons you are assigned an advisor at the beginning of your studies, and it's important to be in contact with him or her each semester.

Just as you applied to be accepted to college, you must also apply for gradation. Lots of students miss this one. Most colleges/universities have two graduation ceremonies, one in the fall semester and one in the spring semester. During the fall semester, the deadline is usually in October. But in the spring semester, the deadline is in March. This is when the Office of the Registrar tallies your course credits for the major you entered to see if everything is in order. Before you send out your announcements for graduation, please make sure you and your advisor have received a notification from the Office of the Registrar that you are indeed graduating. It can be really embarrassing to find out right before the ceremony that you may need to defer to another semester to graduate.

As you move toward graduation, circumstances or emergencies may arise that cause you to withdraw from a class or from the institution as a whole. Check your catalog for the last day to withdraw from a class and to withdraw from the university. Remember, there is always a form to complete for every transaction in college. May sure you keep your copy. Make yourself a file in your room and never throw anything away until you walk across the stage and receive your diploma. That also includes any test or exam papers.

Financial Aid

If you are a student who is receiving financial aid, check with that office before you complete paperwork to withdraw. Your money is affected when you do not complete a semester as a full-time student. You receive your money each semester by the number of hours you have enrolled in. If you are a full-time student, you must enroll in twelve or more semester hours. Part-time students enroll in fewer than twelve hours. If you change your schedule from time to time, make sure you keep the right number of hours required by the financial aid provider. And if you must withdraw from the institution, there are ramifications there as well. Know what they are before you move forward so no surprises are waiting for you in the future. And if you have missed the deadline in either of these instances, contact your advisor. There are plenty of ways to maneuver around this.

Withdrawing from an Institution

If you decide that this institution is not for you, don't just walk away and stop attending. One day you will want to begin your studies again, and if you do not complete the proper paperwork, all your attempted grades will turn into Fs at the end of the semester. And it's difficult to dig yourself out of this hole, especially when it was not necessary. Keep your transcript clean.

Repetition of Coursework

If repeating a course to replace a grade, the course must be repeated at the same institution. You cannot replace that grade by taking it at another institution. Some institutions will limit the number of times you may repeat a course. The most recent grade will be used in meeting graduation requirements.

Independent Study

The need for an independent study comes about when a course that you need is not being offered and not taking it will cause a delay in you matriculating toward graduation. Courses are taken in order each semester, in order to keep you in line for your date of graduation.

By the time this happens, you should be in your major course of study and familiar with your professors, and you should have an advisor in your discipline. Approach your advisor and make him or her aware that a course you need is not being offered and you would like to request that the department allow you to enroll in an independent study. Paperwork, of course, will be needed for this to happen. This means that the department will add the course to the schedule with you as the only student, meaning that you will be assigned to a specific professor who will give you a project during that semester that will equal the credit hours for the course needed.

Your college catalog is a contract between the student and the college, so that if you enroll in the courses they have mandated for you to take each semester, you will graduate in four years. Sometimes a department may have issues that come up that prevent them from offering a required class for a semester, and the student is left in the lurch. If you find yourself in this situation, contact your major department advisor.

Prerequisites

A prerequisite is a course that is required before another course. For instance, English Composition I is required before English Composition II. In a college catalog, courses in your curriculum are listed in the order that you will be registering for them. If you enroll in a course before taking the prerequisite, you will be withdrawn automatically, or the instructor will catch the error and ask you to withdraw. This simple error could cause you a problem. The error could be caught at a time in the semester when it is too late to add another class. This leaves you one class fewer than you are required to complete by the end of the semester. Your financial aid may be affected because of this error.

Class Attendance Policies

Be punctual. Each instructor has a policy on class attendance. Know what it is. Some professors promptly close and lock doors once class begins. That means if you are not there, you are absent on that day. Once you have missed the permissible number of classes for that professor, you will be asked to withdraw from that class. If not, the professor will drop you and award you an F at the end of the semester. If you don't attend, you cannot learn.

This policy is a shock for students coming out of high school, but this is where your maturity kicks in. You must be responsible for your education. This means knowing what is expected of you. On the first day of class, each instructor passes out a syllabus. This document will explain to you what is required of you in order to be successful in this class. Class attendance is a very important part of the class. Read and keep a copy in your files.

Cheating and Plagiarism

Cheating is intentionally using or attempting to use unauthorized materials, information, notes, study aides, or other devices in any academic exercise, such as a test or exam. Plagiarism is intentionally or knowingly presenting someone else's words or ideas as your own. Be careful when you go online to do your research for homework assignments. Instructors know all the tricks too.

Financial Aid Probation

If a student does not make satisfactory academic progress, they can be denied financial aid, meaning, if you are not successfully completing the number of hours you registered for each semester, that can become a problem and result in being placed on probation with financial aid. The college catalog is more specific on the rules per credit hour and per semester. Please meet with the financial aid officer to learn more about how this may affect your progress.

Grade of Incomplete

An incomplete grade is given when a student is unable to complete required work because of an unavoidable circumstance, such as illness. Assigning the I grade is at the discretion of the individual instructor. Meet with each instructor and explain your specific situation. It is the student's responsibility to request the I grade. An incomplete must be removed within one semester, or it will automatically be converted to a grade of F by the university registrar.

Academic Probation

To stay in good academic standing, each semester you must maintain no less than a 2.0 grade point average.

If you fall below the required 2.0, you will be placed on academic probation. This means you will be given a limited time to increase your grade point average or you will be placed on academic suspension. This means you will be suspended for one semester and must apply for readmission after the semester.

Online Courses

Freshman students are not ready to enroll in online courses. These are courses for students who are disciplined, organized, and ready for this responsibility. These are courses that are strictly online. You must log in on time, complete assignments on time, and make sure assignments reach the professor on time. If you forget, have computer problems, or do not complete the assignment before the assignment is no longer available, you will fail the course. Instructors accept very few excuses.

Online education has become very popular with adult students. Online classes offer unprecedented success, and learning outcomes compare favorably to those of face-to-face settings.

Students think online courses are great because they can complete the course online at their leisure and are not required to attend classes. Beware!

Social Media

Please be aware that one day you will apply for a job, whether it's while you are in college or after you graduate.

Watch what you place in your emails so that it won't keep you from securing a job or cause embarrassment. Don't place a picture with you sitting on the toilet with a forty in your hand and using expletives. Job recruiters, whether you know it or not, look at many places to research the characteristics of their next employee. Be careful.

Resources

Writing Lab

Students can work here independently on their writing or with a consultant who is available to answer questions or provide suggestions while they write. It's a great area to brainstorm ideas for your paper or make revisions on your draft.

Math Lab

Tutors are available to assist you but will not do your work. Instead, they will help you identify the available resources and ask you questions to help guide you through the learning process. Always come prepared with questions.

Career Center

The career center is a good place for looking over jobs in your major area, including where they are and what the salaries are. You can also find aptitude tests that show what type of personality you have and information about how to interview for a job, dress for an interview, and write a résumé. There are workshops and seminars and information about studying abroad and internships. They will encourage you to be in control of your career development.

Disability Services

This office assists students with special health conditions. You must provide documentation of your disability and request the appropriate services. You will need these services at the beginning of the semester, so it is imperative that you file paperwork prior to the deadline so that your services will be in place when needed. Make yourself aware of the disability documentation guidelines by visiting this office and meeting the staff. You will meet with this office every semester with your class schedule so that your needs will be met in a timely manner. Don't procrastinate. Seek them out early.

Transfer Office

This office has articulation agreements with many four-year institutions. These agreements contain information about what courses or programs will transfer from a two-year school to a four-year school.

If you plan to attend a two-year school and transfer to a four-year college, this office will track your courses for that particular school and advise you each semester and then assist you when it's time to transfer to make it as smooth as possible.

Distance Learning

If you work and are not able to attend traditional classes, and you do not need the structured classroom setting, then distance learning is available to you through online courses. But you must have the knowledge of how to use a computer and software, and you must be capable of uploading and attaching files and navigating the internet using a browser.

Make sure you check the guidelines for this program and ask plenty of questions about how to be successful using distance learning.

Counseling Services

Sometimes you may feel overwhelmed, depressed, or not happy, and you need to speak with a professional. Well, this office is where you head. Counselors are available to college students for times such as this. I made sure my Freshman Seminar class toured this office each semester. A lot of times, you just want someone to listen. This office is also great about sharing with you the consequences of drinking and drugs. This is very prevalent in our colleges and universities, and if you have questions, they have answers.

PART

II

Advice for Parents of College-Bound Students

Let's talk! Maybe this is your first student about to head off to college. Or maybe your student is the first in the family to attend college. Or maybe your student is in high school, planning to attend college in the future. Having a conversation with your student and planning are necessary. I have four children myself, and the greatest advice my parents shared with me was "Each is an individual; don't compare one with the other." One son completed a four-year university. One son completed a two-year college, and a son and daughter enlisted in the armed services upon high school graduation. Of course, my dream was for all four to earn a four-year college degree, but their career choices were different from my expectations. They all decided which direction they wanted their lives to travel and followed the trails that were provided to achieve their goals.

I have met several parents during my tenure in higher education who wanted to direct their students into *their* career choices. You can't live out your life through your children. Either you will be disappointed or they will be miserable. Just because your family was full of doctors or lawyers does not mean your children will follow their lead. Encourage them early on to think about what they would like to spend their lives doing. And then encourage them to do their research on what it takes to enter those careers.

Before your student enters the ninth grade, he or she must decide whether or not he or she plans to attend college. If so, make sure your student is on the college track. This means that he or she will be enrolling in high school courses that are required for entrance into college, either a two-year or four-year. I listed these classes earlier in this book. In high school, some students enroll in fluff courses instead of courses that will challenge them. Those fluff courses will not gain entry into college.

Follow your student each semester and look at the classes he or she is advised to enroll in, and by all means, ask questions. Remind the teachers and counselors that your student is bound for college.

While in high school, select colleges that you and your student are interested in. Take time to visit the schools of your choice if possible. And by all means, check to see if the colleges on your list include the major your student is interested in. You would be surprised to know that some students select a school because of their athletic teams or because he or she happens to like the school colors. No kidding. Many students have selected a school and found out later that their fields of concentration are not offered at the institution.

While in high school, if your student enrolls in Advanced Placement classes, make sure you retain the records of the results of their scores from the College Board. The scores will indicate if your student will receive college credit for the AP classes completed. The results of these scores must be submitted to the registrar's office prior to your student enrolling in his or her first classes. Why? Because if your student has received a score that will give him or her credit for biology, then you would not want an advisor to enroll your student in biology that first semester. If so, you will be paying for a class that your student has already received credit for. I have seen this happen many times. The registrar will receive a copy of the results and file them away. But unless you bring attention to those results, it may be too late by the end of the first semester of college.

Also while in high school, make sure your student learns how to study and understands the purpose of time-management skills. Some students go to college not knowing how to study or manage their time, and believe me, they will need these skills in college. Students tell instructors all the time, "I never had to study in high school. My parents woke me up every morning, and I never had study time at home. But I made it to all my athletic practices."

Parents, please discuss with your students how to manage their time and the importance of studying. So much will be thrown at them their first semester of college that they may become overwhelmed or frustrated. College professors expect students to be prepared for college once they enroll, and that is far from the reality. They expect students to know how to read and comprehend, write, discuss, think, study, take exams, manage their time, and a multitude of other things, along with going to class each semester. Usually, by the time students have caught on to all of this, a year has passed them by, and they are looking at their first set of grades, which, by the way, does not come through the mail. So, don't camp out at the mailbox at the end of the semester, waiting for grades. Grades are submitted into your student's online account, which each student is given at the beginning of his or her first semester. And your student will submit a password to enter the account. Get that password so you can log in and know the grades. But beware, once your student has shared the account with you, he or she may change the password again. You must know all the tricks, and there are many.

Be on Time

Promptness is another area lacking for many students. They feel they can arrive late for class and be admitted. Wrong. Instructors will close or lock the door when class begins, and if you are not in your seat, you are absent for that day. Some students seem to feel college is a continuation of high school. In high school, the bell rings to signal time to move to another class. Parents get them out of bed in the morning before leaving for school. "I can do my homework at any time or not at all." No time is set aside for studying. Everything is hit or miss.

Students who are not used to structure arrive at college and are confused, lost, and all over the place.

Class Attendance

Your student must understand that class attendance is mandatory. Each instructor will hand out a class syllabus on the first day of class. The syllabus will have all information that the instructor will cover the entire semester, along with exam dates and homework assignments and project due dates. And most importantly, it will include how many classes a student can miss before he or she must withdraw from the class. Once a student has missed that number of classes, the instructor can withdraw him or her or insist that the student withdraw. This is a policy.

This means that the student will not earn the credit hours for that class, and if the student is receiving financial aid, it will affect that. Remember, the grades and the money go hand in hand. If a student doesn't make the grade, the money goes away, which is why the student must attend class.

Attitude

"Your attitude determines your altitude." One of my main topics with students is this quote. The many offices on college campuses have concerns about the awful attitudes that students display when seeking information or assistance. The language is atrocious, and the English is no better, which leads to the need to know how to communicate.

Communication

Have a conversation with your student about the proper way to communicate with adults. Some feel it is the same as speaking with one of their buddies. Courtesy and respect are required in college. Students are required to respect one another as well as respect one another's property. There are rules and policies in place to make sure that happens, and you don't want your student to end up on the wrong side of that type of situation. Part of communication is listening. Your student must know how to listen too. There is a difference between hearing and listening.

Reading and Writing Comprehension

Make sure, before your student leaves high school, that his or her reading and writing skills are up to par for entering college. A vast amount of students struggle with not being able to comprehend what they have read, and this can be a frustrating setback in college. Resources to assist in such areas are not readily available in college because students are expected to have this knowledge upon entry. You can encourage reading and writing at home, beforehand, at no cost.

Dress

You would think this is a topic that does not need to be discussed. But at one of my institutions, I had to discuss with students, young ladies especially, how to dress appropriately for attending college. Students would come to class with see-through clothes, very short skirts, mini shorts, and blouses with a neckline so low that everything was about to fall out. And some were dressed like they were going to the nightclub. It was so bad that a dress code had to be established. Of course, the young men enjoyed it, but this is not why we go to college. Their issue was the sagging pants, so I taught them what a belt is and how you use it. And I kept some on hand in my office, along with safety pins for young ladies to pin together their low necklines.

If the instructor felt that the attire was distracting in class, the student ended up in my office. That meant the student missed a class worth of material that would not be made up.

Responsibility

Is your student responsible enough to handle college life? It's up to him or her, because you won't be around. Students must communicate on their own in order to handle their day-to-day business. Are they afraid to talk to adults or authority figures? Do they know how to figure out where to go for what? Have their lives been structured enough to know how to prioritize, manage, and resolve issues? Are they too proud to ask for help?

Resources

Ask for help soon! There are resources available to students, like the writing center and the tutoring center. Make sure they know to ask for help soon and are not afraid to ask for assistance. If they wait too late, playing catch up doesn't always work, especially when the majority of the semester has already passed by. The instructor is also a resource. That should be their first point of contact when struggling in a subject.

Financial Aid

It would be a great idea for your student to check out where the financial aid office is located and meet the financial aid advisor in charge of the account. The advisor is usually assigned by your student's last name. Then, if any questions arise during the semester, your student will know exactly who to see.

As I have stated before, the money follows the grades. If the grades are fine, the money will continue to be available each semester, but if students do not meet the required number of hours per semester, financial aid will be affected. Your student should seek advice *before* withdrawing from classes. Students enrolled in twelve semester hours are considered full-time. Fewer than twelve hours a semester is considered part-time. If your student is a full-time student, he or she must be enrolled in no less than twelve semester hours, and if they withdraw from a class that results in less than twelve hours, financial aid will be affected. Your student must be responsible for keeping up with the dates and times of when he or she can or can't make changes to the schedule. It is understood that situations will arise, like illness and family emergencies, but your student must be aware of the policies that govern those circumstances.

Early College High School

High schools have joined with two-year and four-year colleges in establishing *early college*. Students begin in the ninth grade and earn a high school diploma and complete two years of college credit. Students that possess the maturity and independence to accept the challenges of this progressive school are capable of honors-level work and can participate in college classes. Parents should contact a middle school counselor about this program.

Family Educational Rights and Privacy Act (FERPA)

My child is attending college, and I am paying the bills, yet when I call the campus, no one will talk to me about my child.

At each freshman student orientation, I spoke with parents separately from the students and shared with them information that would calm them down about leaving their students at college and how to be in the know about their students once they returned home.

The Family Educational Rights and Privacy Act came about in 1974. The long and short of this act is that the student must give proper consent for disclosure of his or her record or academic information. It will not be released to anyone unless that proper consent is given. And that includes parents.

If you call the institution to talk with the financial aid office about a financial status, or you call the registrar's office about grades, you will be told that that information cannot be discussed with you. If you try contacting an instructor, you will receive the same results. And that normally sends parents into a tailspin.

Each college or university has a form titled "Student Release of Information" or "Student Consent to Release Information," or something along those lines. Each school will call it something different, but they will know exactly what you are talking about and may be surprised that you know about this form. The catch is *you* cannot request this form, because it does not require your signature. So, take your student aside and send him or her to the registrar's office to request and sign that form. You cannot go and request this form, because your student is an adult now, right?

It's good to handle this when you bring your student to orientation, along with all the other business that you are taking care of. It will give you a great sense of peace. These forms are filed in the Office of the Registrar, so that when a parent phones the institution, they can say,

"My student has a release form filed," giving them the right to information. They will check to see, and then you are good. Now, one other thing. Sometimes this form is good for only one semester, and your student may need to sign another one in the future. But now you know the secret!

Conclusion

Most colleges enroll many students who aren't prepared for higher education. In this book, I highlight problems that cause students to spend six years in college and leave with no degree. A high school diploma doesn't guarantee that students are prepared for college courses. Institutions of higher education spend time and money to attempt to get those students up to speed or risk losing them. When remedial courses are added to college-level requirements, that means more time and money while taking courses that are not required for graduation. This adds to student frustration.

Even many who pass state high school graduation tests show up to college unprepared. In the "Hechinger Report," Sarah Butrymowicz states that the percentage of students who graduate from high school without the skills they need to succeed in college is so high. Research has shown that students who enroll in these remedial courses often never even make it into the classes that will count toward a degree. Nearly half of entering students at two-year schools and a fifth year at four-year schools were placed in remedial classes at the point of entry.

The majority of these students failed to complete their remedial classes.

Another big problem among college students is they don't know how to study. Most will tell you they never studied in public school, so they expect to use the same technique in college. Wrong! But this is easily and inexpensively fixable before the students walk onto campus.

Most students have never been taught how to study, and the strategies they devise on their own don't work. First-year students typically study less, write less, and read less than they thought they would. Both students and institutions must share the responsibility for this sad state of affairs.

The other side of this is the nontraditional student. Remember, this is the student with the responsibility of working a job, taking care of a family, and balancing all of this with attending school. Fitting in time to study may be an issue, especially if you are taking too many classes. Think about all your responsibilities before registering for classes each semester. A good rule of thumb is to study two or three hours per credit hour per week. If you're taking fifteen credit hours this semester, you should expect to spend thirty to forty hours studying each week. The College Board even suggests that you should think of college as a full-time job, in which you spend about forty hours a week in class, labs, section meetings, and study groups and doing homework.

Students don't like to read, and when they are required to do so in college, it's usually a chore. Reading comprehension is closely related to this issue.

Most students don't leave college for financial reasons, as stated before. And research suggests we can easily and cheaply address the problems that prompt them to quit.

Another weakness is poor planning. Left to their own devices, students don't plan, and even when professors require them to plan, half don't know how to.

With all of these factors, students might get discouraged, but a student who is the first in his or her family to attend college, or a minority, may construe the experience as evidence that he or she is not college material.

It is amazing that students make it through twelve years of school without learning how to study and manage their time, as these issues could have been addressed in middle or high school.

What does it take to be really ready? According to Partnership for 21st Century Skills, "Students will need to be able to think critically, and solve novel and complex problems, be able to communicate to diverse groups and across varied types of teams, take initiative in their own learning, be confident that they can meet their goals through hard work and persistence, and be well-balanced, socially and emotionally savvy people overall."

Earlier, I mentioned a big black book with the huge letters NACADA that looked like it was a hundred years old. Well, after doing some research back at that job, I discovered those letters stood for National Academic

Advising Association. Needless to say, I became a member immediately to learn how to become a professional academic advisor, according to the standards and guidelines in higher education.

After joining this organization, going to conferences, and learning with others at institutions across the country, I became an academic advisor so that I could assist my students. Being a professional academic advisor includes a lot if you do it correctly. This is why some are not always good advisors; it requires so much of them. An academic advisor helps students in the following ways:

- selecting the correct courses before registration
- not enrolling in early-morning classes if they aren't early-morning people
- knowing their learning styles versus the teaching styles of their instructors
- knowing their strengths and weaknesses in subjects required
- remembering the resources that are available to assist with their studies
- making sure they enroll in the correct number of classes per semester to satisfy their financial/ scholarship requirements
- making sure their class schedules are not rearranged before checking with their advisor and financial aid
- remembering the deadlines each semester for when they are allowed to withdraw from a class or the college

- remembering the consequences of each choice they make
- knowing the academic policies and major/program requirements

For the above situations to take place, there must be a student-advisor relationship, which is sometimes equated to a patient-doctor relationship. This advising relationship has shown to increase student satisfaction, retention, and graduation rates.

My years of advising students has inspired me to write this book. My passion for advising and helping students achieve success is still alive and well, as I currently work with students and parents in the community to encourage them along the way.

Bibliography

Butrymowicz, S. "Most Colleges Enroll Many Students Who Aren't Prepared for Higher Education." *Hechinger Report*, September 14, 2016. https://hechingerreport.org/colleges-enroll-students-arent-prepared-higher-education/.

Cominole, M., and Radford, A. "Understanding Today's Student Demographic: Key Questions and Answers." December 2, 2015. https://evolllution.com/attracting-students/todays_learner/understanding-todays-student-demographis-key.

Gates, G. "Ten Common Problems Students Face in College." December 2, 2015. https://owlcation.com/academic/common-problems-for-college-students.

Kuh, G. "What Student Data Tells Us about College Readiness." *Peer Review* 9, no. 1 (2007). https://aacu.org/publications-research/periodicals/what-student-engagement-data-tell-us-about-college-readiness.

Ross-Gordon, J. "Research on Adult Learners: Supporting the Needs of a Student Population That Is No Longer Nontraditional." *Peer Review* 13, no. 1 (2011). https://aacu.org/publications-research/periodicals/research-adult-learners-supporting-needs-student-population-no.

Sharp, J. "Are Students Really Ready for College, Work and Life?" March 14, 2017. https://www.gettingsmart.com/2017/03/students-really-ready-college-work-life/.

Strauss, V. "A Telling Experiment Reveals Big Problem among College Students: They Don't Know How to Study." *Washington Post*, September 14, 2016. https://www.washingtonpost.com/news/answer-sheet/wp/2016/09/14/a-t … a-big-problem-among-college-student-they-dont-know-how-to-study/.

Sun, C. "First-Year Reflections." *Peer Review* 8, no. 3 (2006). https://www.aacu.org/publications-research/periodicals/first-year-reflections.